CONTENTS

Dedication	4
Carry on Sarah	5
From Spirit To Spirit	8
Confused	11
The Miner	12
The Missing Watch	14
The Tramp	15
Out of The Dark	16
Lost Teeth	18
Wallpapering	20
Keeping Fit	22
Conversation	24
A Blizzard	25
Autumn's Change	27
Respect	29
The Love of My Life	30
A Countryside Scene	31
The Gardener	33
Bonfire Memories	35
Holidaymaker's Nightmare	37
Accident	39
Growing Up	40
Brixham does care	41
Dartmouth	43
Looking to rest	45
Results of Surgery	47
Cherry	50
My Garden	52
Courting	53
A Sunday Walk	54

Facing Life with A Smile - *by Beman*

Dedication

I would like to dedicate these poems to Carole my late wife of 47 years To Laura Turner who looks out for me And Sarah Howard who along with Laura has helped me turn my life around for the better.

God Bless Them

SARAH

FACING LIFE WITH A *Smile*

☺

Beman

MAPLE
PUBLISHERS

Facing Life with A Smile

Author: Beman

Copyright © Beman (2025)

The right of Beman to be identified as author of this work has been asserted by the author in accordance with section 77 and 78 of the Copyright, Designs and Patents Act 1988.

First Published in 2025

ISBN 978-1-83538-890-7 (Paperback)
    978-1-83538-891-4 (E-Book)

Book cover design and Book layout by:
    White Magic Studios
    www.whitemagicstudios.co.uk

Published by:
    Maple Publishers
    1 Brunel Way,
    Slough,
    SL1 1FQ, UK
    www.maplepublishers.com

A CIP catalogue record for this title is available from the British Library.

All rights reserved. No part of this book may be reproduced or translated by any form or by any means, electronic or mechanical, including photocopying, recording or by any information storage and retrieval system without written permission from the author.

The views expressed in this work are solely those of the author and do not reflect the opinions of Publishers, and the Publisher hereby disclaims any responsibility for them.

Facing Life with A Smile - *by Beman*

Carry on Sarah

After the loss of my wife
I decided to get on with my life
To do the garden and clean
But it was all too much
For a disabled man as such

With weeds growing unneeded
Inside a woman's touch was needed
It all got me down
Dusting needed all around

One day I could see
A young lady pruning a tree
She worked hard with pride
It looked good from my side.

She asked could I move my car some more
To sweep leaves from the floor
I said, "Yes that's fine.
Could you do mine?"

To cut the lawns
Prune the shrubs
Clean the borders
Everything she could.

My joy soon showed
Seeing my lawns mowed
Flowers began to show
Some growing high, some low

Facing Life with A Smile - *by Beman*

She filled bin after bin
With garden waste and weeds
Cuttings, weeds, unwanted seeds
Unwanted plants all went in

Then rain came down, it poured
I asked if she would do indoors
Again she agreed
One thing I really did need.

We got on well
In a friendly way
She tells me off
Don't know who's boss!

Cleaning tiles
Vacuuming carpet
Mopping floors
Dusting doors.

Making beds
Wiping window ledge
Bathroom sink and toilet clean
Kitchen same, she is supreme.

She is more like a sister
An adopted daughter
She now is a friend
Someone I can depend upon.

How did I manage without her
She is reliable and honest
She worked hard and was shy
Now a friend, who I can rely on.

Facing Life with A Smile - *by Beman*

In the garden she comes alive
Pruning edges and shrubs
Mowing lawns
Weeding borders and tubs

I like people who work with pride
Both in the garden and inside
We became friends from the start
A Yorkshire pair not too smart.

My life has improved
There's a new beginning
At last, I can feel
That now I am winning.

Thank you from my heart Sarah
You have helped change my life!

Colin

From Spirit To Spirit

He came home late
In a drunken state
His wife in despair
Marriage beyond repair.

A wife with no hope
Starts crying once more
Could no longer cope
She showed him the door.

Swearing he walked out
They both began to shout
Leave her, he must
After a breakdown of trust.

He wandered onto a railway track
Stumbled and fell onto his back
Between the lines he lay
Why had life turned this way?

With a feeling of remorse
As he headed for divorce
With his senses coming back
As he lay on the track

If he could keep off drink,
He began to think
And give a better life
To his once faithful wife.

Facing Life with A Smile - *by Beman*

Once his life was fine
They shared good times
He would go back and see
If she would listen to his plea

He then rolled over
From his back
As he heard a train
Coming down the track.

Thinking that was close
As the train went past
He then passed out
On a large patch of grass.

He woke up in the light
Though he thought it was night
He went to search for his wife
To promise a new life.

He was now dressed in rags
Under his eyes lay big bags
He was not aware
How long he had been there.

He wandered back
Saw his wife dressed in black
With a large, flowered spray
She was heading his way.

He said hello
But she just walked past
She did not seem to hear
He felt an outcast.

Facing Life with A Smile - *by Beman*

She met his old friend
Outside the church gate
They went to a grave
Her and his old mate.

He looked at the grave
Where he saw his own name
Was this all a dream?
A puzzle it became.

Then a bright light
He began to see
He then thought
Did that train really miss me?

Confused

Just out of bed at eleven
"O O"

Can't sort a problem out
Maybe you'll know.
I employed a gardener
Then asked her to clean
I am her boss and feel very
Mean.

Now the cleaner who is my Gardener
Has become a good friend
Where will it all end?

Now my friend who is also
My gardener
And my cleaner has become
Part time helper.
She says that makes her my
Boss.

Just can't sort it all out
Confused.

The Miner

Every morning,
At half past four,
A miner leaves home,
Locking his kitchen door.

He walks down the street
With an echoing sound,
His wooden clogs beating
On the ground.

He collects his helmet,
His lamp, and number tag,
Which he places
In his bag.

He then travels
In a cage,
Down a shaft
To earn his wage.

A very proud man
Trying to earn a living,
Knowing the coal face
Can be unforgiving.

High humidity,
Dust and coal,
Chewing tobacco
To reach his goal.

Facing Life with A Smile - *by Beman*

A creaking roof,
A fall of dust,
Toil and sweat—
He knows he must.

Stripped to the waist
And shovelling coal,
A dust-covered body,
A hard-worked soul.

The end of a shift,
A time to laugh,
A welcome shower
At the pithead bath.

Then home to rest
His aches and pain,
Knowing that tomorrow
It's the same again.

Facing Life with A Smile - *by Beman*

The Missing Watch

My wife shouted out "Hurry up, we are late".
It was our thirtieth anniversary date.
"I cannot find my watch," I said in some shame,
The reply came back "It's always the same."
"When you do get ready on time,
We never are quite so late as this time."
I looked in the drawer, on the shelf, on the table,
I looked everywhere that I was able.
But now my long-cherished dread appeared,
I had lost my watch as I had feared.
"Hurry up!" she shouted sounding quite mad,
"It was a gift," I said feeling quite sad.
A watch had been given to me,
On our last anniversary,
Again, going over where I had been,
But my watch was nowhere to be seen.
I walked to the car, my mind in a twist,
Then noticed the watch was on my wrist.

The Tramp

I saw this man come down the street,
His shoes badly worn upon his feet,
His clothes all dirty, and in tatters,
Looking as if he no longer mattered.

He was carrying what I thought was a bundle of rag,
It turned out to be his sleeping bag.
His eyes glazed in a motionless stare,
His face half covered in thick matted hair.

His trousers were tied by his belt and shoelaces,
He did not have use of any fancy braces.
What made this man look so forlorn,
With his clothes all tattered, and torn?

Could it be because of all our greed?
That's taken away what these people need?
I gave him some food, and a drink of tea,
His face lit up full of glee.

Then he left but I would see him no more,
How could this man have become so poor?
I felt quite sad and a little sorrow,
Wondering what would become of him tomorrow.

Facing Life with A Smile - *by Beman*

Out of The Dark

At the end of the tunnel
I could not see a light.
No bright blue sky,
Only darkness at night.

My tunnel had no start,
I could see no end.
It was full of twists,
Sharp turns, and bends.

No flowers or birds,
No fields of green.
No leaf-covered trees,
Anywhere to be seen.

A thick cloud of fog
Blinded my sight.
Lonely I had become,
Future days not so bright.

Then you came along
And ended my strife.
Now a tunnel full of love
Has entered my life.

You opened my eyes,
You removed my fear.
I hear birds sing,
I can see clearer.

Facing Life with A Smile - *by Beman*

I see blue sky,
A guiding light,
Twinkling stars
On a clear moonlit night.

Leaf-covered trees,
Meadows showing green,
A myriad of flowers
Everywhere to be seen.

To share my new life,
I would like you to stay,
To be my partner
Until my dying day.

Facing Life with A Smile - *by Beman*

Lost Teeth

While tending to my plants,
On a hot sunny day,
I planted some of them out.
Where they were to stay.

An ice cream I was offered,
Then realising what I had done,
I'd lost my two false teeth—
O' where had they gone.

To the dustbin I did run
But in my great haste,
I simply had forgotten.
They'd just been taken away, the waste.

I looked into the dustbin,
Which was quite empty now,
Then beads of sweat began to form.
High up on my brow.

The compost bin was next.
To come into my mind,
But my two front teeth,
I really could not find.

Now I felt quite desperate,
And drained by the sun,
It just had not been my day,
I was not having fun.

Facing Life with A Smile - *by Beman*

I now began to think,
Forever I'd lost my teeth,
I even moved the compost bin.
To look right underneath.

Had the dustmen taken them,
Had they fallen in the bin,
By now I started to regret
I had not kept them in.

I now searched all around the house,
I also searched it in,
Conservatory, and plant pots,
I'm now in quite a spin.

Then walking up the garden,
My mind was in turmoil,
I glanced down and saw my teeth,
There lying on the soil.

A rubber from my walking stick
Was also on the ground,
The day before I had lost it,
But now it had been found.

After cleaning up my teeth,
I can now sit with a smile,
With my walking stick repaired,
I can walk for many a mile.

Facing Life with A Smile - by Beman

Wallpapering

The bedroom we had started to decorate,
The wallpaper we got, we got it quite late.
We could not agree on the bedroom décor,
My wife picked the paper I thought was quite poor.

She brought home the paper, she knew she would win,
If there was an argument, I would soon give in.
As she went out shopping, I thought of a surprise,
I'd put on the paper before she would arrive.

I began to paper the bedroom wall,
I'd even a stool; I found it was too small.
I stepped off the stool but, in my haste,
I put my right foot in the bucket of paste.

My foot real sticky as it went right in,
Just as the telephone began to ring.
A trail of paste I left on the floor,
As I answered the phone behind the front door.

"Wrong number," said the man who had made the call,
Turning back, I slipped down the hall.
My right foot gave way and then I fell,
While someone was ringing the front doorbell.

Our friends saw me lying there on the floor.
By the time I got up, I was so sore.
"I've come to see your wallpaper," she said,
The lady next door with a large grin.

Facing Life with A Smile - *by Beman*

I cleaned up the mess, myself as well,
By now it was hard, you just could not tell.
After this I finished the room,
It did not seem a minute too soon.

My wife came in, we had a drink,
Then she said, "Do you know what I think,
As I lay thinking in bed last night,
I've begun to think you were quite right,
That paper I bought is not what I like."

Keeping Fit

I went to the sports centre.
To try to get fit.
First a swim, then a sauna
To relax and sit.

Into the sauna
I did walk,
Leaving my wife
To have a good talk.

As I closed the door
I felt my back twist,
Then pain down my legs—
It was a slipped disk.

Lying down
I tried to shout,
But the words
Would not come out.

Full of pain
I tried once more,
By this time
I lay on the floor.

My wife and receptionist
Just could not hear,
They kept on talking
Oblivious to my fear.

Facing Life with A Smile - *by Beman*

By now my back
Felt like a fire,
I was feeling weak.
And beginning to tire.

The ladies kept on
Having a good chat,
About him and her,
And this and that.

I first turned pink,
As I lay on the floor.
Then bright red,
Sweating more.

By now the conversation
Got louder it seemed,
No one could hear.
My frantic screams.

I managed to drag
Myself to the floor,
And find enough strength.
To open the door.

It dragged my body.
To where they both sat,
While they were both
Still having a chat.

Then the receptionist,
With a horrific stare,
Turned to me and said,
"We forgot you were there."

Conversation

Everything is black and white,
With nothing in between,
That's the view of my wife,
Or that's the way it seems.

Intelligent conversation
Just ends in my dismay,
It seems when my wife is wrong.
She turns it the other way.

While sometimes listening to her speak
And feeling rather amused,
I suddenly find the tale has changed.
I really get confused.

Sometimes when I talk to her.
It really is quite queer,
I feel I'm talking to myself.
She just does not want to hear.

I sometimes tell her bits of news.
That I have overheard,
Later then she tells it back.
Repeating it word for word.

It seems that I will never learn,
And do not take it in,
That where my wife is concerned.
I really just cannot win.

A Blizzard

Evenings of darkness,
Ghostly sight of the moon,
A cold whistling wind
Brings a feeling of gloom.

Winter is here.
Weather changes at pace,
The sleet and the rain
Blow cold in my face.

The bleak country lane
At this time of year,
Where I must walk
Reduces me to fear.

Into the raw wind
I struggle to walk,
My nose cold and red,
I'm too cold to talk.

I arrive home from work,
First sight is the fire,
A bath and hot meal
Is what I desire.

Next morning from my window,
A picture postcard scene,
A blanket of snow
Covering fields that were green.

Facing Life with A Smile - *by Beman*

Icicles from gutters
Hang down from my house,
Warm breath on the windows
Drifts out from my mouth.

Drips of cold water
Outside of my door,
Drops from the icicles.
Fall onto the floor.

The cold spell of winter
Little warmth from the sun,
With snow on the ground
The children have fun.

But I dream of spring.
And lighter nights,
Trees turning green.
And flowers in my sight.

Facing Life with A Smile - *by Beman*

Autumn's Change

A leaf of golden brown
Falls without a sound,
Then leaves by the thousands.
Carpet over the ground.

Leaves yellow, red, and golden.
Now shed by the trees,
Fall all over the countryside.
And blow about in the breeze.

Seeds from the sycamore
Propel down to the ground,
Horse-chestnuts and acorns drop,
With a gentle sound.

Squirrels frantically bury.
Their nuts under the ground,
Hopeful that after their rest,
They can easily be found.

From dawn until dusk
Busy farmers plough their fields,
Hopeful next year's harvest
Bumper crops will yield.

After summer's showy blooms
With flowers past their best,
Some plants just wilt and die,
Others go to rest.

Facing Life with A Smile - *by Beman*

Longer spells of darkness.
Less daylight can be seen,
Morning frosts start to cover.
The last shades of green.

With weather now changing,
Sometimes looking quite grim,
Seems like everything is waiting.
For winter to set in.

Trees looking like skeletons.
After losing summer's show,
The hedgerows look quite lifeless,
Where once they did grow.

Autumn starts off glowing.
Brilliant colours at their best,
It leaves us with nature.
Prepared for winter's rest.

Respect

Respect is a thing we both give and take,
Lack of respect is a grave mistake.
Respect like a present, is quite free,
The giver and taker need not pay a fee.

It's easier to say, "Thank you, good morning, are you well?"
Than to try and make people's lives seem like hell.
Respect is steadily drifting fast,
Like a sum of a crime, it is bound to decay.

We all should think what we do wrong,
Weak minds don't care; caring minds are strong.
Greed and selfishness are what this brings,
Respect for people as they grow old.

To ask for respect, a handout of gold,
Shows that respect a person has sown in need.
Of friends because of feelings insecure.
His miseries have gone, weight-loss no more,

To worship money and material things,
With no respect what deep sorrow that brings.
Rich men respect less than the normal wealth,
For the loss of respect is greater than health.

Respect of mind is better than social wealth,
For the loss of respect is quite plain to see
With the breakdown of society.

Facing Life with A Smile - *by Beman*

The Love of My Life

When I first saw
The love of my life,
I hoped and I prayed.
She would become my wife.

Despite a distance of many a mile,
Nothing could distract me.
From her loving smile.

Once we had married,
We shared highs and lows,
We bonded together
And made our love grow.

Now still together
In our later years,
We face many challenges.
And share all our fears.

The feeling I felt.
When I first saw my wife,
Is still the same feeling.
For the love of my life.

Facing Life with A Smile - *by Beman*

A Countryside Scene

I view a picture on my wall.
A tranquil scene but that's not all,
Although that picture looks quite well
A different story I can tell.

I stare then I begin to dream.
Of walking by that twisting stream,
Walking under arching trees
Listening to the rustling leaves.

Rays of light shine through the leaves
Gently changing with the breeze.
A medley of music comes from the birds.
Whose mating calls are loudly heard.

A well-worn path of clay and slate
Formed by travellers as of late,
The earth and shale that form the lane.
Has worn out hollows formed by the rain.

Roots of trees hang from the hedge.
Like an enlarged spider's web.
Insects scatter all around
In the hedge and on the ground.

Looking for a place to hide
Dashing away from my side.
Scent from flowers a fragrant smell
Drifts down the lane into the dell.

Facing Life with A Smile - *by Beman*

Through gaps in hedgerows can be seen
A patchwork of fields
Yellow, brown, and green.

Hedgerows with flowers thickly spread.
Poppies galore a brilliant red.
The path then weaves on down the hill.
Leading to an old watermill.

The air I breathe it tastes so pure.
Like sparkling wine left to mature,
The way I feel is quite at ease.
Walking in the gentle breeze.

My mind alert, then at rest
While viewing the countryside at its best,
But realising it's only a dream.
I gaze once more at the countryside scene.

Facing Life with A Smile - *by Beman*

The Gardener

As winter passes with the start of spring
And birds in the trees start to sing,
The crocus and daffodil start to flower,
A garden job beckons for every hour.

From dawn to the last daylight,
Even beyond and under false light,
Our labour we start to deploy,
But a time we greatly enjoy.

With digging the vegetable plot and planning done,
Thinking of the meals yet to come.
On bad days I sow flower seeds,
Always too many for my needs.

When small plants start to emerge,
I feel my adrenalin start to surge.
With the vegetables, herbs and flowers
Taking up many unpaid hours.

Hard labour I sometimes need to deploy,
With a feeling of achievement, I really enjoy.
Great pleasure I get as I plod on,
Laughs also come as things go wrong.

When bad weather tries to spoil my fun,
Jobs like potting up can be done.
After cutting the lawn and raking out moss,
And chasing off cats that dare to cross.

Facing Life with A Smile - *by Beman*

Plants shaped and pruned one by one,
The weeding, watering and feeding all done.
I share my garden with the birds and bees,
And people passing by it seems to please.

Then as the summer sun starts to shine,
My garden matures like a rich, sparkling wine.

Facing Life with A Smile - *by Beman*

Bonfire Memories

On the fifth of November
Was Guy Fawkes' gunpowder plot,
They filled Parliament with explosives.
And tried to blow up the lot.

King James was the target,
Year sixteen hundred and five,
But the failed conspirators
All paid with their lives.

We now burn an effigy.
On the top of bonfires,
Built of timber and trees.
And sometimes old tires.

We eat roast potatoes,
Sometimes pie and peas,
Followed by treacle toffee
Washed down with warm tea.

With a display of fireworks
White, red, blue and green,
Rockets flying high,
A sight to be seen.

People stand in awe.
Looking into the sky,
Changing shapes and colours
Are pleasing to the eye.

Facing Life with A Smile - *by Beman*

Hands held up in front
Getting warmth from the fire,
People watch excited children.
Who never seem to tire.

When the fire burns down
To the last burning ember,
Leaving time to reflect—
A time to remember.

Facing Life with A Smile - *by Beman*

Holidaymaker's Nightmare

One summer's day in Brixham
While flying over the Strand,
A seagull released
Its waste to the land.

Jim wearing shorts only,
Sat eating chips, it is said,
Was unfortunately splattered.
Over his shiny bald head.

He hastily looked up
Towards the bright sky,
Only to be hit,
This time in his eye.

People passing by,
They looked, some did grin,
Some cheekily pointed
To what had happened to him.

By now Jim's face,
Spotted white, and bright red,
He swore and he cursed,
"I'll kill you!" he said.

Facing Life with A Smile - *by Beman*

To dispose of soiled chips,
He tried a waste bin,
But the bin overflowed,
He could not get them in.

He went into a rage,
Threw his chips on the ground,
Then saw scores of gulls.
Appear all around.

The gulls squawked and fought,
Jim kicked and he screamed,
All hell had broken loose.
Or so it seemed.

With the chips and gulls gone
Jim was left feeling mad,
He now looked dirty,
Disgusted, and sad.

A lady shopkeeper,
Offered him a damp cloth,
So that he could wipe
All the bird messes off.

A passing fisherman said,
"You're in the wrong place,
Look up at King William—
They've near covered his face!"

Facing Life with A Smile - *by Beman*

Accident

I never tried to fall
It just happened to me
I tried hard to recover
But never got free.

It shows no respect.
For the way I felt
I was never very happy.
With the hand I'd been dealt

But how people have
Helped me
Brought a tear to my eye.
A lump in my throat
I wanted to cry.

My pain never eases.
My illness won't part.
But seeing people happy
Still touches my heart.

I try to make people.
Happy
To forget their woes
This gives me pleasure.
More than anyone knows.

And always remember.
People worse than me
May need help.
For a life that's stress free.

Growing Up

I was once a child
Loving to shout
Carefree and wild
Running about

No violence or hate
To turn my mind
Everyone was my mate
Loving, helpful and kind

Bad language was not heard
Graffiti was not seen
Did not know a bad word
The streets kept clean

Respect was not bought
Not like today
You would be caught
If you did not obey

The penalty for sin
Used to fit the crime
Life made quite grim
For those in decline

Now money has replaced God
Sin is the norm
It's called being mod
Not like when I was born

Facing Life with A Smile - *by Beman*

Brixham does care.

We called in for coffee
At Brixham does care
We found two ladies
Looking on in despair

"They closed Paignton theatre"
oh what a mess!
"We are struggling to cope"
One did confess

With queues to the door
They could not believe
As they stood at the fore
It was hard to conceive

The queue just got longer
But they did their best
Not getting any stronger
They yearned for a rest

"I could do with a fag"
Jean called out to Joan
"I've some in my bag"
Jean said with a groan

But these two ladies
Stuck to their task
They carried on serving
What more could we ask

Facing Life with A Smile - *by Beman*

We are lucky to have
people so rare
With John and the rest
Showing Brixham does care

Facing Life with A Smile - *by Beman*

Dartmouth

Packed with tulips
Opening for the bees
Pale pink blossom
Hanging from the trees

Springtime in the park
Has come at last
The dreary winter
Seems long since past

A beautiful bandstand
Stands with such pride
In a large paved area
To the front and the side

The lawn and hedges
Look quite pristine
With borders of flowers
Filling in between

Plenty of benches
Where people can meet
Can sit and relax
Those weary feet

Sitting by the river
Watching the ferries
Feeling calm and relaxed
Forgetting any worries

Facing Life with A Smile - *by Beman*

Blending with buildings
Of a bygone year
Town and old market
Situated quite near

The river Dart
Flows fast and wide
With views of Kingswear
On the other side

The naval college
Sits on a hill above town
Where King Charles
Trained on the grounds

Facing Life with A Smile - *by Beman*

Looking to rest

With a book
And the sea in mind
I travelled to Brixham
For a relaxing time

Walking down fore street
On the pedestrian road
I was almost knocked down
By a passing skateboard

When reaching the harbour
I could not believe my luck
There an empty bench
Where I could read my book

I sat on the bench
Looking out to the sea
A mother and child
Sat next to me

The child was screaming
The mother shouting loud
We looked like a family
To the staring crowd

Feeling embarrassed
I looked up to the sky
Then a seagulls motion
Hit me in the eye

Facing Life with A Smile - *by Beman*

Then leaning on railings
Close to me
I felt a breeze
Saw my hat in the sea

Next the harbour wall
I instantly fled
When a child sat above me
Dropped ice cream on my head

I decided back home
Was the best place for me
I arrived back
To the smell of my tea

So into the back garden
With my book and a chair
I sat relaxed
In the fresh air

Results of Surgery

I sit in a wheelchair
And stare at the walls
I sometimes try walking
But it all ends in falls

Surgeons operated
Half way up my spine
Three operations I had
Left me paralysed last time

I refuse to give in
And don't feel depressed
And hope I will triumph
As I try for success

Doctors prescribe drugs
To ease all my pain
But I find small relief
As it comes back again

Sometimes I feel
I am winning the fight
Other times I know
I will never be quite right

I remember the effect
It first had on me
It felt like a cramp
I just wanted to be free

Facing Life with A Smile - *by Beman*

Ten years later
On crutches I go
With limited distance
I walk very slow

I refuse to give in
As I feel it's inept
To be as I am
I will never accept

Whenever I can
I laugh and I smile
Try to be like others
If only for a while

I try not to burden
Others with my fate
They have their own troubles
They try to escape

My whole life altered
It's not the same
I find doing somethings
I had to re- train

Challenges daily
Come to the fore
As I master each one
Then look out for more

People help me a lot
I find most are kind
As I search for a solution
That proves hard to find

Facing Life with A Smile - *by Beman*

I've adapted my life
And do other things
The harder the challenge
More contentment it brings

I study the problems
I face day to day
I study them hard
Till I find a way

I look back on life
I feel no remorse
Cause whatever we do
Nature will just take its course

Facing Life with A Smile - *by Beman*

Cherry

Cherry is the serious one,
Her faults are hard to find.
She is very conscientious,
But can also speak her mind.

She is the considerate one.
Who will always share her time,
She will always take the lead,
Leaving you safe behind.

She's very outspoken.
But fair in what she says,
Her trustworthy nature
Stands out in many ways.

A typical agony aunt,
Who listens to us moan,
She gives you back your confidence,
So, you don't feel alone.

A lover of animals,
With a heart of gold,
She will give them all her love.
Or so that's what I'm told.

She will do anything for anyone,
And organise their day,
So, everything runs smoothly,
In every single way.

Facing Life with A Smile - *by Beman*

She will analyse your problems,
Advising you with care,
She will tell you what is wrong.
So, you are well aware.

I hope this poem brings a smile.
To your bright red cheeks,
I know that you will tell me off.
The next time that we speak.

I hope that you will not change,
I like you as you are.
You helped me through my darkest days,
To me you are a star.

JEN

Facing Life with A Smile - *by Beman*

My Garden

The sun shines high above us all
Casting shadows on the wall
A dog barks wanting to go for a walk
Wonder what he'd say if he could talk
Sheep bleat on a hill over the way
The other side horses answer with a neigh
Ants scatter over paths and drives
Carrying cargo way over their size
A bee buzzes around looking for a flower
That's full of pollen he can devour
He flies in and out of plants with speed
To pollinate them to make seed
The flowers in all their colours grow
Some bushy, some climbing, some high some low
They sway around in the gentle breeze
Blending in amongst the trees
Along come the insects, beetles, slugs and snails
Some flying, some running, some on slimy trails
The Blackbirds and Robins come in for their food
They pull out worms that dare protrude
With Finches and Blue tits flying around
Wagtails wagging their tails on the ground
A smell from the herbs, honeysuckle and sweet pea
Seems to drift over the garden to me
A frog's eyes stick out from the garden pond
Another one croaks behind a stone beyond
Pleasures like these if you are aware
Can be seen free, sitting in a garden chair

Courting

You've never kissed me
Or got close on the settee
You never once held my hand
To make me feel rather grand
You never talk
When out on a walk
You never show any passion
Must be out of fashion
Your clothes never change
Which seems very strange

Won the lotto by the way
I'm leaving you today
Stop talking and listen
Stop squeezing my hand
I don't understand
Stop kissing my lips and face
It's only a waste
Put your clothes back on
We are in a busy street
Heeelp!

A Sunday Walk

My walk taken on Sunday
Took me up a hill
Up to the churchyard
Where all seemed quite still

I sat on a seat
Near the entrance gate
I looked at the graves
Of the people of late

Some gravestones were leaning
From erosion of time
They looked weather beaten
And covered in grime

The path to the church
That stood there quite proud
It was made of stone paving
Worn down by the crowds

Who attended the service
And visited to pray
Mostly on Sundays
Which is sabbath day

Large trees all around
New graves with fresh flowers
The church bells rang out
From the bell tower

Facing Life with A Smile - *by Beman*

As I sat there
I started to dream
About life gone by
And what people had been

Villagers earning a living
Varied work earned their pay
Laughing, joking, gossiping
All characters in their way

There were rich men
Who thought only of gain
Then there were poor men
With a life lived with pain

Good times and bad times
Most had to face
Now sons and daughters
Have taken their place

Some friends and relations
Are laid here to rest
Apprenticed in life
Till they passed their test

Each life had a story
A different life to tell
Some. made mistakes
Others did quite well

Until time had come
When they no longer would arise
Their last breath had been taken
They had last closed their eyes

Facing Life with A Smile - *by Beman*

They came here for christenings
Then grew up from a child
Those days of great joy
As they ran around wild

This place was the place
They stood here with pride
They stood arm in arm
With their loving bride

Now at their end
These people god blessed
Their minds now at peace
Their souls are at rest

www.ingramcontent.com/pod-product-compliance
Lightning Source LLC
Chambersburg PA
CBHW052120070526
44584CB00017B/2569